CHASING APPLE
TO FIND JERRY

ALEXIS REED

For my mother Lorayne, for teaching me how to make a way out of no way.

CHAPTER 1

I never really had a desire to know my father when I was young. His given name was Jerry, but he'd been nicknamed "Apple" as a kid due to his apple-shaped head. He was also referred to as "Crazy Apple," a title often accompanied by the speaker's widened eyes and hushed tone that let me know, even as a kid, that something wasn't quite right about him.

My parents were together from their teens to their early twenties, and had two children during their decade-long romance: my older brother Tyrue, and me. My mother told stories of a good boyfriend and father who, over time, had transformed into an obsessive, abusive, and violent person. She eventually ended the relationship, and the rumor went that their breakup had literally driven my father to insanity.

Throughout my childhood my father was mentioned periodically, but I was really only ever reminded of his existence when Tyrue voiced his disappointment about another football game he'd missed.

At thirteen years old, my brother was the star of any team he played for, as his speed, agility, and sheer competitive drive made him the perfect football player. Tyrue was popular both on and off the field—he'd walk around our Maryvale community with a crowd of friends by his side, radiating an aura of pure, magnetic charisma. At five feet five, with an athletic physique, beautiful smile, and ebony complexion that glowed under the Arizona sun, Tyrue's likeability was undeniable.

I received all the perks that a little sister with a well-known, loving big brother could expect. I was oftentimes served candy for breakfast, compliments of either Tyrue or his best friend Paul, and any time our nearby playground's swings were all taken, it wasn't long before one became unoccupied if my brother was around. He'd lead me over to it with a reassuring grin, and soon I'd be gripping its warm steel chains, pumping my feet back and forth while looking into the cloudless, bright blue Phoenix sky. I was his beloved baby sister and he protected me to the fullest, even taking the blame and disciplinary swat a few times when I'd done something wrong. I'd ride on the handlebars of his blue ten-speed mountain bike, holding on tightly to keep my bottom from sliding off as Tyrue wove through our neighborhood's cars and the wind whipped past my cheeks. We'd scream with laughter, and I was never afraid to fall—not really, because I knew that if I did, my brother would catch me before I hit the ground.

I didn't really long for a father because I had my brother, who I never doubted would be there for me whenever I needed him. It wasn't until the summer of '97 that my confidence in Tyrue's comforting presence was shattered, when he was sent to prison at fifteen years old for grand theft auto. Unbeknownst to our family he'd gotten involved with a gang, and on the day he was apprehended, he'd run from the police to my aunt's house. My mother went and retrieved him, and Tyrue immediately led me, our two younger half-sisters, and our half-brother to his room.

"I want you all to hold hands," Tyrue requested, tears streaming rapidly down his face.

We did as we were told, clasping our tiny, shaking hands together.

"I've done some bad things, and I have to leave for a while," Tyrue began, and I shook my head in disbelief.

"No. No! You can't go," I said, lips trembling. "I need you here."

"Shh," Tyrue said, gathering me close for a tight, familiar embrace—one I wouldn't get to experience again for several years. "It's going to be okay."

At the end of the day my brother turned himself in to the police, was tried as an adult, and received a three-year sentence in Florence's maximum-security prison. I was only twelve years old, and my brother's absence was devastating at first. The lack of a solid male figure impacted me greatly, but it wasn't until my freshman year of high school that the thought of reaching out to my father crossed my mind.

It was all because of a questionnaire, with one line that read, "What is your father's occupation?" I skipped over it, going on to add my mom's information instead.

"Very nice, Alexis," my teacher said later, scanning my answers. "Your mother works in social services? That's great. I used to as well."

I pursed my lips and nodded, silently imploring her not to ask about the blank spot on my questionnaire.

"But I see you didn't fill out your father's occupation?" my teacher continued, blinking her beady brown eyes at me.

"Um…" I started, wringing my hands under my wooden desk. "I don't really know anything about my father."

"Wouldn't you like to?"

I gave my teacher a nonchalant shoulder shrug. "No. Not really."

"Hmm." She was done with me after that, bustling over to the next student with a smile—probably because they'd filled out both of their parents' occupations.

My teacher's innocent questioning stuck with me long after she'd shuffled away, and that same day I went home and asked my mom if I could meet my dad in person.

"Any particular reason?" she asked from where she stood in front of the kitchen sink, quickly hiding her shock behind her long black braids.

"We were talking out our fathers' occupations today at school, and I had nothing to say," I answered quietly, hoping this wouldn't upset her.

My mom turned her attention back to the dinner she was making and agreed, stating she'd arrange it as soon as possible.

• • •

"Now if you feel uncomfortable or scared at any time, let me know and I'll come get you," my mom said on the way to visit my dad.

"I think it should be fine," I said, staring out the window at the rolling thunderheads approaching from the north. It was monsoon season, and I loved the summer storms with their thick, grey clouds and warm, fragrant rain perfect for playing in. I was fourteen years old, and the oncoming storm helped to calm me as I prepared to meet with my father for the first time that I could remember.

As we pulled up to a house I'd never seen, I saw a shorter guy pacing back and forth in the front yard. He was dressed in blue jeans, a black shirt, and black sneakers, with a complexion of the deepest, darkest chocolate color. *We have something in common already,* I thought, peering down at my own skin as I opened the car door.

When our eyes met, my dad greeted me with the biggest smile I'd ever seen. "Hey babygirl!"

"Hey Daddy," I said into his shoulder as we embraced. It felt natural, like we were old friends reuniting. My dad looked to my mom where she sat in the driver's seat, his smile becoming a bit more wooden.

"Coffee?" he offered, hope pulsing in his eyes.

"No thank you Apple, I have to run."

"Oh, okay," he said, stepping away from the car. My mom gave us a little wave before driving away, while my dad ushered me inside his home.

As I entered my dad's apartment, I was greeted with the familiar aroma of brewed coffee that instantly made me feel like I was at home. I scanned the front room, noting that the space had the resemblance of a thrift store's decrepit used furniture section.

"Um, Daddy?" I murmured, elbowing him softly. "Your stuff, it's all...mismatched." I pointed to the tattered, mud-colored couch pushed up against the furthest wall, strips of silver masking tape placed haphazardly across its cushions to keep the couch's yellow innards from spilling out. Next to the couch was a battered recliner that I immediately decided I would never sit in.

"This furniture was donated to me," my dad said proudly as he settled into the couch's sagging middle.

"Oh," I said, perching on the edge of the cushion beside him so that the smallest amount of my rear possible touched its stained, torn surface. "So you're the 'less fortunate?' Like those people we pray for at dinner?"

My dad grabbed my hand with a booming laugh. "Well, I guess so babygirl. I guess I am."

After the tour of his place, my dad pointed to a brown wooden chest in the corner of the living room. It was about a foot long, with chipped paint on the sides.

"Go ahead babygirl," my dad said excitedly, leading me closer to the small chest. "Pick whatever you'd like out of my treasure chest!"

He lifted the lid and I sifted around its contents aimlessly. *I'm fourteen, not four,* I mused, searching through jump ropes, plastic bracelets, and little balls in various sizes for playing catch. *Why would I want any of this?*

I reluctantly picked up a pink plastic bracelet, sliding it onto my wrist. "Thank you Daddy."

My dad shook his head, reaching into the chest. "Oh no, babygirl, I want you to have something you can play with!" He selected a blue-and-white package with a small, red rubber ball and a set of jacks. "Here, open it!" My father ushered me to the floor with him, explaining the game of jacks in a rush. I sat there and listening to the rules attentively, pretending I was just as thrilled as he was.

As we finished up our game, my father began to reminisce on my childhood. "Babygirl, do you still like Snickers bars?"

"Yes, I do," I said, putting the tiny metal jacks back in their package.

"When you were little I'd feed them to you all the time!" my father said with a chuckle. "Boy, you used to eat those up, don't you remember?"

"Yes," I responded, although I had no recollection of that.

"The next time you come, I'll have some for you."

"Okay Daddy. Thanks."

The visit with my father wasn't as scary as everyone had made it out to be, but I decided I didn't want to see him anymore after that. Our odd encounter with the gifts had struck a chord of rejection within me, one that I couldn't ignore. To my teenage mind, I figured he'd just gathered a bunch of junk in his free time, not finding me worthy of anything more meaningful. I mean, he'd known I was coming—why not get me a nice necklace or even a card with heartfelt words that said something like "I'm sorry for missing out on your life," or "Let's start over?" Nope; I'd gotten a pink plastic bracelet, ball and jacks, and stories about me eating Snickers bars. Little did I know that it was all he was capable of giving me at the time.

Going forward I limited our interactions to phone conversations, ones that usually consisted of my father speaking obsessively about my mom, who he referred to as "sweet, sweet Lorayne," and jabbering on about when he'd been a kid. He'd nicknamed me "Muffins" by that point—for what reason I didn't know—and our talks would be a jumbled mishmash of topics, with my father speaking rapidly as I tried to keep up.

"Muffins?" he'd say loudly into the receiver.

"Yes, Daddy?"

"You know what I want right now?"

"No. What?"

"Some of Mrs. Juanita's cooking. She sure can cook!"

Juanita was my maternal grandmother, and had helped to raise my father when he was young. My parents' families had grown up on the same street and were very close, and it was something my father mentioned frequently. After asking about everyone in the family, he'd return to his favorite subject: my mother. "You know, you know, me and your mom are getting back together. We're going to work it out."

"Oh yeah?" I'd reply jokingly. My parents hadn't been together for over a decade, but I continued to let him dream.

"Okay Muffins, I have to go now," my dad would eventually say, citing the need to do some grocery shopping or an impending visit with a friend as his reason for ending the call.

"Bye Daddy."

"Hey, hey," he'd say, "it's not goodbye. It's see you later. All right?"

I'd laugh, enjoying the rare moment when my dad's lucidity shone through and he seemed almost normal. "See you later, Daddy. See you later."

CHAPTER 2

Three months after our reunion, I went several weeks without hearing anything from my dad. It was my fall break from school, and I wondered what he was doing for the holidays and figured I might invite him over for Thanksgiving dinner.

I retrieved my phone and dialed my mom's work number, which I'd memorized since she was always there. "Do you know where I can find my dad?" I asked when she picked up.

"If you haven't heard from him in a while, check the prison system. He's been in and out of jail last I heard," she said, sounding distracted as the rings of many other phones echoed in the background.

I frowned and thanked my mom, hanging up and grabbing my laptop. I plopped on my bed and started to search the inmate database online, typing his name into the search bar.

Bam! There he was.

All I could think was *wow*—he was at least fifteen pounds lighter in his mugshot, and his hound dog eyes were bloodshot, red, and full of despair. He looked so sad and pathetic, and my chest clenched as I scrolled through to see what he'd been incarcerated for.

Underneath the big, black lettering that read "CRIME," it stated he'd been picked up for criminal trespassing.

That's not too bad, is it? I wondered. *A little weird, but not bad.* I picked up the phone and called my mom again.

"Hello?" she asked in her formal work voice, before I announced that it was me.

"So he's in jail for trespassing," I said quietly.

"Well that's no surprise," she answered with a snort.

"Uh, yeah it is. Why would he be trespassing?"

"He was probably sleeping outside on someone's property."

"What? Why would he be sleeping outside?"

"He's homeless from time to time."

"That's crazy," I murmured, telling my mom thank you and hanging up again. I grabbed a pen and paper from my desk and began to write my dad a short letter, still processing everything I'd just found out as I retrieved my wallet from my purse.

> *Dear Dad,*
>
> *How are you? I found out you were in jail online. If there is anything I can help you with, let me know. I'm sending you $20.00. I hope it helps.*
>
> *Love,*
> *Muffins*

It was just before Christmas that I received two letters in the mail. One from my father, addressed "Jerry James," and another from a "Jerry Long."

Who's that? I wondered, opening my dad's letter first.

Hey Muffins!

Yeah, I'm in jail. Hey, thanks for the money, how is my Lorayne doing? Tell her to come see me. Hey, listen, my pal that I share my cell with is looking for a wife. I told him you would be great.

I dropped the letter on the table with a cry and immediately called my mother. "Mom!" I yelled when she answered.

"Hello? What?"

"He gave my information to his cellmate!"

"Who? What are you talking about?" my mom asked, flustered by my apparent rage.

"My *dad*!" I cried, angrily crumpling up his letter and tossing it in the trash along with Jerry Long's.

"Well if you're going to continue to write to him, I'd suggest getting a P.O. box," she replied, not sounding the least bit sympathetic. "Is that it? Because I have to get back to work."

"Fine. Bye," I said, abruptly ending the call and vowing never to write to my dad again.

• • •

Three summers went by before I tried to reach out to my dad once more.

I was eighteen by then, and had given birth to two daughters, Alexandra and Aubrey, who I wanted him to meet. Just as before, though, I didn't know where to find my dad. I checked Maricopa County's online inmate database and didn't see him listed there, so I called my mother.

"Contact Magellan Healthcare," she instructed, sounding surprised that I was asking about him again after several years of disinterest. "It's where he goes to get medical services when he's homeless."

Calling Magellan turned out to be a dead end, as they were unable to give out patient information. I understood the importance of HIPAA and confidentiality in the healthcare field, but still felt a little hopeless about how I'd find him, especially with no known last address.

Two days later, my mother called and told me she'd spotted my father in South Phoenix pushing a cart down the street.

"How is he?" I asked, trying to keep my voice level.

She paused, and my pulse quickened. "Not good. He's lost a lot of weight, and he was wearing jeans with a ton of holes in them. No shirt, and his sneakers looked ready to fall apart…"

"Did he recognize you?" I realized it was a dumb question the moment after I asked it—my dad would never forget his beloved Lorayne.

"Yes he did. I gave him some money and bought him lunch."

"That's good. Thanks for helping him."

"I'll always help him. I'd never drive by and not acknowledge him," she said, sounding a bit hurt. "I still care about your father, even if we're not together."

"I know…" I said, immediately guilty for assuming otherwise. "What *happened* to him, Mom? Why does he act this way?"

She sighed loudly into the phone. "He wasn't always like this, Alexis. He used to work and take very good care of us. One night he went to a club, and we think someone put drugs in his drink that started this whole mess. After that night, he slowly began to change."

"'Change?' How?" It was the first time she'd willingly volunteered these details, and I suddenly wanted to better understand this man who'd left our family when I was a baby.

"First he got paranoid, constantly accusing me of cheating. He even set his childhood home on fire during one of his rages. He kept me from my family, and then he started getting violent. That's when I left."

I blinked as I listened, experiencing all sorts of emotions at the confirmation that my father had physically abused my mom. I was disgusted to know she'd endured that, but I still felt a duty to reach out to my sickly, struggling father. After hanging up with my mom I decided to search for my dad where she'd last run into him, and see if I could be of any help. As a safety precaution I asked my boyfriend Stephon to accompany me, and we chatted as we drove slowly through the busy streets of East Phoenix.

"How do you look for someone who's homeless?" I asked, squinting out the passenger side window. "I mean, not to be funny...but do you look around dumpsters? Under freeways?"

"I was thinking we could start here," Stephon answered, maneuvering our car into a Circle K parking lot.

A group of bums were sitting cross-legged near a trashcan in front of the building, and they stared at us when we approached. There was an older black woman with matted grey dreadlocks and a thick winter coat wrapped around her scrawny shoulders, with a cardboard sign that read "I'm hungry" resting in her lap. The man to her right was white, with very blue eyes and a medium-sized brown dog lying beside him. The third bum, a black man wearing a green beanie and dark hoodie, rummaged noisily through a plastic bag as we came to stand in front of them.

H-hello," I stuttered, clearing my throat. "I'm looking for my dad. He's a short, dark-skinned guy named Jerry—Jerry James. Have you seen him?"

"No...I don't know a 'Jerry James,'" the woman replied, while both men nodded their heads in agreement.

My mind raced, and I scrambled to think of more questions. "What about someone named 'Apple?' Know anyone who goes by that name?"

Both male bums laughed, and a flicker of hope grew in my chest. "Oh yeah, I know Apple! Apple Jack? Crazy Apple? Yeah, we know him," said the bum in the green beanie.

"He just left," continued the woman, pointing across the street to a dingy 7-Eleven. "Check over there."

"Great, thanks," I said, turning back toward our car.

"Hey, do you have any spare change?" said the bum with blue eyes, unfolding his long legs to stand.

I wanted to show my appreciation for their help, so I nodded. "Yeah, just one sec." I reached for my purse but Stephon stopped me, pulling his wallet from his pocket instead.

"I'll get some change," he said, returning with fives for each person.

"Thanks for your help," I repeated with a smile, reaching for Stephon's hand so that we could walk over to the 7-Eleven.

The man in the beanie waved at us before we got very far. "Hey, hey, wait! Can I go home with you?"

My blood instantly boiled at his audacity. "What'd you just say?" I barked, preparing to unload a string of profanities in his direction.

Stephon kept leading us away, wrapping an arm around me as he spun to face the bum in the beanie. "No, you can't."

"I want those five dollars back," I hissed as Stephon and I stood on the sidewalk, waiting for the light to change so we could cross the street. "*And* I want to cuss him out."

Stephon squeezed my shoulder gently. "I know Alexis, but he's a bum. His life is already shitty—just let it go."

"That's not an excuse!"

"Listen, if I were a bum I'd want to go home with you too," Stephon said, winking at me and waggling his eyebrows.

"That's gross," I said, wrinkling my nose as a smile broke across my lips.

"Is it? Is it gross?" Stephon said, tickling my sides. "So you wouldn't sleep with me if I were homeless?"

"No!" I said between my giggles, jogging away from him across the street.

Stephon followed and quickly caught up to me, lacing his fingers through mine. "Cheer up, babe. Let's find your dad."

• • •

As we drew nearer to the 7-Eleven, I recognized my dad right away. He didn't notice us at first, and I was relieved to see he looked better than how my mom had described him. He was clean-shaven and sitting by the side of the building, rolling a cigarette on his jeans and singing to himself.

When we were a few yards from him I realized my dad wasn't singing—he was talking to himself. "Yeah, that's me," he mumbled, before laughing loudly. "Yeah, yeah," he went on, still unaware of us. "Just let me get a beer."

When I was near enough to touch him, I reached out and gently grazed his shoulder. "Daddy?"

He jerked away, staring up at me with incomprehension. I studied his irises, and they looked yellowish under the 7-Eleven's fluorescent lights.

"Muffins?!" my dad finally uttered after several seconds of silence. He jumped up and hugged me so tightly that I smelled the body odor wafting off his clothes. "Hey babygirl! You came to see your ol' dad."

"Yeah, I did," I said, retreating a bit once my father had released me from our embrace. His gaze swung over Stephon, and his features immediately darkened. "Who's this motherfucker, Muffins?"

My heart dropped. Stephon stood six feet tall to tower over my father, and was at a much healthier weight. He extended his hand out calmly to shake my father's hand. "I'm Stephon, Alexis's boyfriend."

My dad stared at it, then pumped Stephon's arm enthusiastically. "Oh shit, Muffins! I've got a son-in-law!" He hugged Stephon as well then, before backing away to study my boyfriend. "Muffins, he's kinda big…if he gets out of line, you might have to pistol-whip him."

Oh my god! I screamed inwardly. *What's happening right now, why would he say that?* It was definitely time to go. "All right Daddy, I was just checking to make sure you were okay." I dug inside my purse and extracted a twenty-dollar bill from my wallet, before handing it to him.

My father lightly pushed my hand away. "Oh no, Muffins— I'm not taking money from you and my son-in-law. I'm a straight arrow now, I've got a place to live—"

"Oh really?" I interrupted with surprise.

"Yeah, yeah. I'm just visiting here, I'll give you my address."

My dad proceeded to tell me the information, which I typed into my cell phone. After my dad threatened to end Stephon's life once more if he hurt me in any way, we said our farewells.

"I love you Daddy," I said, giving him another hug.

"I love you too Muffins—oh, and you too, son-in-law."

Stephon grinned. "Take care, Jerry."

"Bye," I said, tucking my phone in my back pocket.

My dad *tsk*ed and placed his rolled-up cigarette behind an ear. "Muffins, remember—it's not goodbye. It's see you later."

I bobbed my chin in understanding. "Of course. See you later Daddy."

Chapter 3

M y dad called me the next day.
"Hey Muffins, it's me!" he crowed into the receiver when I answered.

"Hi Daddy," I said, caught slightly off guard but happy to hear from him.

"Hey, babygirl—um, have you heard from Vanessa?"

Vanessa was another one of my many half-siblings; we shared a dad, but had different moms. "I talked to her earlier today."

"Will you come visit me, and will you bring Vanessa with you? I want to give you guys some money. Bring her with you please."

"Okay," I agreed, ending the call with my dad and dialing her number. "Nessie? Dad just called, and he wants us to come and visit him."

Vanessa said she would, so the next day I drove to her house and we decided to walk to our dad's place together. He lived about three blocks away from her, and it was April so the weather was nice. Vanessa was a year older than me, and we'd met for the first time during a family reunion a decade earlier when I was ten. We'd been inseparable ever since, and shared a lot of our father's physical attributes: broad noses, large eyes, and petite frames.

In all other ways, however, Vanessa and I were opposite—I was introverted and kept to myself most of the time, while she loved to crack jokes in the middle of a crowd, reveling in the many compliments from admiring boys who loved her wild, curly hair.

The walk to our dad's took about fifteen minutes, and when we made it to his street we saw him pacing outside with a coffee in one hand and a cigarette in the other.

When he caught sight of us approaching, he waved. "Hey girls!"

"Hey Daddy!" we replied in unison.

"I'm so glad to see you girls, you're so beautiful, that's that James blood running through you, don't ever forget that," he chattered, embracing each of us and dropping a bit of cigarette ash on my arm. "Oh! I have some money for you girls," he went on, setting his coffee on the porch ledge and digging in his front pocket. He unearthed a wad of crumpled bills, giving us both three twenties each.

"Thank you Daddy," I said, smoothing out the bills on my palm.

"Yeah, thanks, I was super broke," Vanessa added.

"Well, Dad's here to save the day! Come on, let's walk to the store so I can get more cigarettes."

We headed off toward the nearest convenience store, while our dad regaled us with stories about mine and Vanessa's younger years. She and my father did most of the talking while I trailed silently behind, listening to their recollections and the dinner plans they wanted to make for the near future.

Vanessa began to tell our dad about her mother, who had a history of drug addiction. When we made it to the store, we each got a bag of chips and a soda, while my dad bought a beer and some cigarettes. On our way out of the store, Vanessa suddenly stated how neglected she'd felt by our dad and her mom when she was little, and coils of dread knotted and slithered in my gut. We stood on the street corner waiting for the light to change so we could cross, and my dad tapped a cigarette out of his new pack and lit it.

Vanessa retrieved one from her own carton, and my dad offered to light it but she declined.

"Daddy," she said, flicking open her lighter and holding the flame to the cigarette's tip. "*Daddy.*"

Oh no, I thought, concerned by Vanessa's accusatory tone. *This isn't going to be good.*

"Yeah?" my dad finally answered, still puffing on his own cigarette.

"I want to know why you weren't there for me," Nessie said, inhaling a final, long drag before flicking the butt into the street.

My dad stared at Vanessa blankly, before leaning in real close to her face. "I don't owe you a *fucking thing,*" he hissed, his eyes bloodshot and cruel.

He leapt off the sidewalk, darting into oncoming traffic and nearly getting hit by several cars as horns blared all around us.

"DAD!" I screamed, but my father had already disappeared amongst the buildings on the other side of the road.

Vanessa sat down on the curb, holding her head in her hands as she began to cry. I shook with fury—it was the first time I'd ever seen my strong, confident sister break down like that.

Comforting people was admittedly not my strong suit, but I had to try. I squatted down beside her and rubbed her back, extending a hand to help her stand. "Hey, quit crying, Nessie.

Fuck him. Come on; get up. You had to know that conversation wasn't going to end well."

Nessie sniffled and wiped at her red-rimmed eyes. "Fucking asshole."

I grabbed her pack of cigarettes and took one out, requesting her lighter and handing her another lit cigarette, its end glowing orange-red against the oncoming dusk. "We don't cry over men, even when they're blood."

I pressed the button for the crosswalk and we waited until it indicated for us to go ahead. On our way to the other side of the street, we passed the cigarette back and forth in silence.

"Why do *I* have to have the fucked-up parents?" Vanessa eventually muttered, glancing at me.

"I don't know." I wasn't sure what else to say; with an absent father and a drug-addicted mother, Vanessa certainly had one of the most difficult situations I could think of. At least I had my mother, who'd always provided a safe and stable home environment. It wasn't fair.

"It's probably best he wasn't around, Nes. Look at how he just acted!" I pointed in the general direction our father had run off in. "That's not what a dad's supposed to do! Did you see how he just ran out into traffic?!"

"That *was* crazy," Vanessa replied, busting out in laughter that I soon joined in on.

"I thought he was gonna get hit by a car for sure!"

"It wouldn't've mattered—it's not like he has any life insurance," Vanessa exclaimed, and we continued to laugh until we were buckled over, both clutching our stomachs.

By the time we returned to Vanessa's house her tears had dried, and her demeanor was much more cheerful. I said goodnight to my sister, devising a plan that night to have revenge on my father for making her cry.

I'll make sure he knows what a shitty person he was for not being in Nessie's life, I thought as I curled up in my bed after tucking my daughters in. *Let's see how he feels after* that.

• • •

I woke up the next morning with a flame in my belly, looking forward to the conversation I planned to have with my father. I picked up my phone to call him, but it began ringing before I could dial.

My mom's number flashed across the screen, and I answered it. "Hello?"

"Hey, what are you doing?"

"Uh," I said, beginning to stumble over my words. "I-I just woke up…gonna get the day started, you know. The usual."

"Oh, okay. How'd visiting your dad go?"

Damn it! I thought. *Now I have to tell her.* "Well…. he ended up saying some really mean things to Nessie, so I'm going to call him and return the favor."

"Why? Why would you do that?"

"Because he made me mad!" I justified, unsure of why my mom was on *his* side. "He was being rude to Nessie. He made her cry."

My other line beeped, and I asked my mom to hold on before clicking over to the other line. "Hello?"

"Babygirl?"

"Yeah?" I snapped, immediately scowling at the sound of my dad's voice.

"Muffins, I need some groceries."

"Sounds like a personal problem," I said, my tone relentlessly cold.

"Can you go to the store for me? Please, Muffins?"

21

"No, I can't. I'm busy," I replied. "Hold on, Mom's on the other line."

"Lorayne? Is it my sweet Lorayne?"

Who else would it be, Daddy? Do I have another mother somewhere? "No, just hold on."

"Okay, Muffins. Tell her we should meet up later, okay? Tell her we should get together for dinner."

"She has plans!" I shot back.

"Oh," he sighed. "Just tell her that I miss her then."

"Okay! Fine," I said, switching back over to my mom. "Sorry, it was Dad on the other line. He wants me to buy him groceries."

"When are you going to get them?"

I balked at my mom's question. "I'm *not*."

"Why?"

"I don't want to. He's annoying and mean and I don't owe him anything."

"You *are* going to get groceries for him," my mom retorted. "And don't treat him like that. He doesn't get to see his family much—it's just you who tolerates him at this point."

I frowned as my mom's words sank in. "Yeah, okay," I finally mumbled, defeated.

"What was that?"

"Fine! I'll get his groceries. Bye."

I clicked back to my dad's line, frustrated beyond measure. "Daddy?"

"Yes, I'm here Muffins!"

"I'm on the way," I yielded. "Make sure you have your list ready or I'm not going."

"Thanks Muffins! See you later."

I exhaled into the phone, attempting to loosen the tension in my shoulders that had gathered during the calls between both of my parents. "See you later Daddy."

• • •

I did my father's grocery shopping that day, and once each month moving forward. Six months later when I was at his place retrieving his list, he asked if he could come along.

"Sure," I shrugged, unlocking the car door for him.

Once we'd shopped in a nearby Safeway for a while and filled the cart, I strode over to the greeting cards section and searched for a birthday card for my best friend.

"I'll grab the rest of the food and meet you up front," my dad said, and I nodded absentmindedly. I kept scanning the cards for several minutes, picking several up and putting them back when the inside message wasn't quite what I wanted. Suddenly, I heard shouting from the front of the store.

"Give me my fucking groceries bitch!" someone screamed, and I froze. *Is that my dad?*

I speed-walked to the front of the store, locating him immediately in the nearest checkout line.

"Sir, you don't have enough money," the cashier stammered.

"Look, I know how much money I have!" my father roared.

I dropped the card and ran over to him, gasping when I saw the register screen. The total was over four hundred dollars, when we'd had a budget of two hundred at the most.

"I'm sorry, I'm so sorry," I said to the cashier, who was near tears at that point. I started grabbing the things we needed and putting them in the cart, leaving the rest on the conveyer belt. Other employees had begun to gather, trying to get us out of the store as fast as possible.

Through my haze of horror and embarrassment, my dad continued to bellow his indignation to anyone close to us. "I am a mathematician, and I don't appreciate this establishment trying to *cheat me out of my money!*"

I closed my eyes and took a deep breath, trying to center myself in the chaos. When I opened them again my dad was shouting about cigarettes, and I walked right up to him and grabbed his forearm firmly. "Daddy. *Daddy.* Look at me."

His bulging eyes shifted to study my face, and he softened. "Hey Muffins. You ready to leave? We can go home and cook some of this food."

"Yes, I'm ready," I said, "let's go."

I directed my dad to the cart and he began pushing it, waving and smiling to the employees he passed.

"I'm sorry again," I said to the cashier my father had screamed at, who was staring in shock as he left through the sliding glass doors, perfectly affable. At that moment, I realized something was terribly wrong with my father.

I was silent on the car ride home, while my dad babbled on and on about my mom.

"Oh Muffins, that Lorayne…she's something else."

"Uh huh," I said, chewing on my bottom lip.

"She drives me crazy babygirl, like a bat out of hell!"

"Yeah, I know," I said dismissively, pulling up to my dad's place. We quickly unloaded the car, and I made up an excuse about having to leave once the groceries had been put away.

"Let's cook next time," I said, avoiding my father's amiable gaze.

"You gotta run?"

"Yes, I do."

"Okay kid," he said. "Thank you. I love you, and I'll see you later. Right?"

I kissed my dad quickly on the cheek, then ducked out the front door. "Yep. I love you too, and I'll see you later."

It wasn't until I'd started the engine that I allowed my tears to surface. "What the hell was that?!" I exclaimed aloud as I drove home from my father's house, gripping the steering wheel with sweaty palms. *What's wrong with him? Why would he do that?*

Dozens of questions ricocheted in my mind, and I knew exactly who to call about them. Once I'd gotten home and taken a shower to calm down, I dialed my mom's number.

"Hey," I said, giving her the rundown on my dad's odd behavior. When I was done she didn't reply for a little while, and I finally had to prod her to respond. "Mom? What's going on?"

"Honey…he has paranoid schizophrenia."

"Schizophrenia? What? I need to look this up," I said, locating my laptop. "Are you sure?"

"Yes, I'm sure. Alexis, he wasn't always like this, so be nice to him. Remember what I told you about those drugs that were put in his drink? That's what changed him, nothing else. He loves you, and you're really all he has now. He's a good man, even when it seems like he isn't. It's not his choice to be like this."

"Yeah, ok," I said, typing "paranoid schizophrenia" into the search bar of my internet browser.

"I'm serious," my mom said, sensing my doubt in her statements.

"Does he have to take medicine for it?"

"He's supposed to go to that healthcare place, Magellan, but I don't think he does. And he probably won't."

I ran a hand through my hair, thoughts racing. "All right, I'll talk to you later."

I ended the call with my mom and kept researching the diagnosis, learning that paranoid schizophrenia was a subtype of the mental illness in which the individual experienced delusions and hallucinations, often taking the form of suspicions that others were plotting to hurt them in some way.

I scrolled through words like "serious disorder," "altered reality," "hearing voices," and "jealousy," but Google grew boring relatively quickly.

When I switched to YouTube, reality hit. I watched it for five hours straight, video after video after video detailing delusions, paranoia, flat affect, emotional withdrawal, chemical imbalances, the onset period, and tons more. I went into a craze that evening, trying to understand everything I could about schizophrenia. I was mentally exhausted by the end of it, and most of all, heartbroken that there was no cure and that my father's reality was a day-to-day nightmare I couldn't fix.

That night I was restless in bed, thinking about my dad's store outburst, his sudden verbal attack on Vanessa, his homelessness, the constant obsession with my mom, and his overall spastic behaviors. It all made sense, and I was overwhelmed by emotion. How could I have been so inconsiderate? When the sun began to crest over the horizon I was still awake, having spent the night sobbing into my pillows until they were soaked with tears.

I just didn't understand. *Why him?* I'd heard great stories about my father, this chocolate man who'd been a great provider, who'd loved his children dearly. The thing was, I'd never met that man—I'd never met the real Jerry. I only knew Apple, "crazy Apple." I began to wonder if pieces of Jerry were still in there somewhere, or if Apple had completely taken over.

CHAPTER 4

The incident at the store had made me wary of my father, unsure of whether he was safe to be around. I'd developed the coping mechanism of avoiding in-person contact with my father whenever I felt overwhelmed, and for the next six months I only communicated with him by phone.

In the fall of 2005, my father called from the Maricopa County 4th Avenue Jail. I was braiding my eldest daughter Alexandra's hair when I heard Stephon accept the call where he was in our bedroom. I finished Alexandra's braid and instructed my daughters to grab a snack while I took a break from doing their hair. I stood in the master bedroom's doorway, regarding Stephon.

"Yes sir, your daughter is fine," he said, rising from his seat on the edge of the bed, "let me hand her the phone."

Stephon covered the phone's mouthpiece and whispered, "He's in for assault, trespassing, and theft."

I nodded in acknowledgment, my heart sinking as I took the phone. "Hey Daddy, it's Muffins!"

"Babygirl! It's so nice to hear your voice. How's my grand-babies?" my dad said, chipper as ever.

"They're fine," I managed to say even as my throat swelled, warning of an impending crying jag. "Would you like to say hi?"

I took heavy steps into the kitchen where Alexandra and Aubrey happily munched on cheese sticks.

"Yes, yes, let me talk to them," my dad mumbled, sniffling audibly.

"Daddy, are you crying?" I asked, keeping my words steady. "Are you okay?"

"I just want to get out of here!" he wailed. "I want to be with my family!"

"Daddy, please stop crying. I'm putting you on speaker-phone with the girls now." I approached the kitchen table and held the phone out, my hand tremoring the smallest bit. "Say hi to Grandpa, girls."

"Hi Grandpa!" they stated in unison.

"Are you girls being good?"

"Yes but Alexandra won't let me ride her bike!" Aubrey pouted.

"Alexandra, always share with your little sister," my father instructed; he'd collected himself enough that his cries were no longer perceptible.

"Alexis—come here!" Stephon hissed from our bedroom. I frowned, setting the phone down on the kitchen table between the girls and walking over.

Stephon had his laptop balanced on his open palm, and pointed to the screen. "I don't think he'll be getting out of jail anytime soon."

"What?" I grabbed the computer and read the information Stephon had pulled up, which detailed that my father's minimum potential sentencing for the crimes he'd committed was three years.

"Mom, we're done talking to Grandpa!" Aubrey soon shouted from the kitchen.

"Coming!" I handed Stephon his laptop and hurried back to the kitchen.

"Thank you girls," I said, taking my phone back and switching it off the speakerphone mode. A warning beep that our time was running out echoed in my ear.

"Hey Daddy, there's only a couple of minutes remaining for the call…"

"I know Muffins; I just called to let you know that I got sentenced this morning, and it's four years."

I had paced into the living room by then, and sank heavily into the nearest chair. "Oh. Oh wow. When will you be released?"

"December of 2009," my dad said, and I was unsure of whether he was crying again.

"That's a long time…"

"It is. But it's okay Muffins; you don't have to worry about your ol' dad. Don't send me money, save it for my grand-daughters."

"Okay Daddy," I forced out, squeezing the fabric arm of the chair with my free hand to keep from breaking down while we spoke.

"I love you Muffins, and my son-in-law too."

"We love you Daddy."

"Okay Muffins. Remember—it's not goodbye. It's see you later."

"See you later Daddy," I said, just as the call was dropped because we'd overstepped our time limit.

• • •

My father's release date came and went, but I paid no mind to it. By 2011 I was working full-time, and had become deeply occupied with raising my daughters, who were ten and eight.

It was in the fall of that year that information about my father once again rocked my life to its foundation.

Cheer season was in full-swing, and Aubrey would keep me company as we sat on our blanket in the school's grassy field, watching Alexandra practice her cheers. Aubrey liked to follow along, imitating her sister's chants, cheers, and jumps. I encouraged her periodically, keeping myself occupied by checking Facebook. I was browsing the posts in my feed when something caught my attention. I stopped scrolling, blinking several times in disbelief.

I'm seeing things, I thought, horrified.

But no—the picture before me was real, too real, of a man standing on a street corner with a desperate puppy-dog expression, his pants around his ankles. He held a cardboard sign that read in nearly illegible handwriting: "HUNGRY."

My hands were slick with cold sweat as I read the caption of the post: "Look at this!"

"This" was my father.

The comments below the photo ranged from disgust to concern to surprise, each one like barbed wire twisting ever more tightly around the vulnerable pulp of my heart.

Why haven't I looked for him in all these years? I wondered, shaking my head as I withered in regret and shame.

My eyes were misty and unfocused when a high-pitched blast from the cheerleading coach's whistle startled me, indicating that practice was over. Aubrey had already returned to our blanket and was munching away on the snacks I'd brought, and I motioned for her to get up so we could join Alexandra. I gathered our blanket and belongings and headed toward my eldest, resolving to find my dad and get him some help as soon as possible.

The next morning I made a few calls, and found my father's new caseworker through Magellan. George informed me that my dad visited their facility every day for medication, food, and transportation, which was a great start in my search for him.

"Does he come in at a particular time?" I asked George.

"Not really. He's pretty unpredictable, and just shows up whenever."

"Okay, thanks."

I grabbed my purse and car keys, rushing out of the house to find my dad. On the way I stopped at a thrift store and bought him some shorts, shirts, and shoes, followed by a dollar store, where I purchased some hygiene products. I went to all the spots where I'd seen my father hanging out, but it was unsuccessful. Next I drove to Magellan's facility, and when I located George, he said I'd just missed my dad by ten minutes or so.

I set the bags of clothes and toiletries down and ran out to the parking lot, scanning the area for a glimpse of my father. When I couldn't find him, I went back inside and watched as George put the items I'd bought into an empty closet.

George scanned me and chuckled at my breathlessness. "Did you catch him?"

"No," I said, slumping into a nearby chair. "Do you know when he'll be back?"

"Nope. He comes when he feels like it, and we just provide him the services when he gets here."

"Damn."

"Why are you chasing him around town like this?"

For some reason I became defensive over George's harmless questioning. "Because I feel like it!"

"Whoa," he responded, "I think what you're doing for your father is great."

"Yeah, *sure*," I muttered, pushing out of the chair.

"He'll be back soon," George said, returning to his computer and rearranging the papers on his desk. "You really don't have to hunt for him."

But I do, I thought. *Who else is going to look after him?* "Can I leave my phone number in case he comes back?"

"Of course you can."

"Do you have an envelope?"

George shuffled around in a drawer, and handed me a crisp white envelope. I stuffed twenty dollars inside and sealed it, then turned it over and wrote him a little note, along with my cell number.

Hey Daddy,

I came and you weren't here. If there's anything else I can help with, just call me. I love you, be safe and stay cool. see you later.

Muffins

The next morning I woke up to seventeen missed calls from my father.

Before I could return them, my screen lit up again and I answered it groggily. "H-hello?"

"Muffins! Get up Muffins! Guess what?!"

"*Daddy?* What? What happened?"

"I got a job!"

"You got a job?"

"Yeah Muffins, I'm a working man now." The pride was undeniable in my dad's voice, and I was thankful to hear how healthy and clearheaded he sounded. "Hey baby, look, I got a job now; I'm going to do a one-eighty, I'm going to turn everything around. I'm going to get a nice house for Lorayne, with everything that she wants—oh, and a big kitchen!"

I rubbed the sleep from my eyes and yawned. "That's great Daddy. Where are you working?"

"Oh, over there at Honey Bear's barbecue restaurant, cleaning the parking lot. Yeah, I took that money that you gave me and washed my clothes so I could be presentable at work."

"That's good Daddy; I'm proud of you." I sat on the edge of my bed, glancing at the clock; it was seven a.m., and I'd have to wake the girls in a few minutes for school. Stephon had already left, since he had an hour-long commute to Chandler from our apartment in North Phoenix.

"Hey Muffins, can you bring me some food for lunch?"

I grinned—my dad knew even after more than six years that I could always be counted on for a meal. "Yes, what would you like?"

"Can you make me some pork chops? And a salad with green onions, cucumbers, tomatoes, and Italian dressing?"

"Sure Daddy. I'll be there around noon."

"All right Muffins. See you later."

"See you later Daddy."

I ended the call and went into my daughters' room, opening the shades to allow the bright white sunshine in. "Good morning girls!"

"Good morning Mom," said Alexandra, who'd already gotten up and dressed herself. "Aubrey won't get up, I already tried twice," Alexandra added, tying one shoe and then the other.

"Is that so?" I walked to Aubrey's bed to find my youngest huddled under her beloved blanket, which she'd nicknamed her "kink kink" as a toddler.

"Aniiiiiiyah," I said gently, pulling the blanket back.

She opened her eyes and looked at me, yawning a sleepy "good morning."

"Time to get up, Cupcake," I said, yanking the covers the rest of the way.

"Why?" Aubrey whined. "Why does school start so early?"

"You're in third grade now," I explained, promising both girls that we could stop at Paradise Bakery for bagels on the way to school.

After feeding my daughters and dropping them off, I I headed home to cook for my father. I'd been working doubles on weekends as a certified nursing assistant, which left my week free and allowed me to prepare and deliver my dad's lunch that day. I began cutting up the veggies and frying his pork chops, and soon had a nice little feast ready for him.

I drove over to Honey Bear's BBQ ten minutes to noon to find my dad right where he'd said he'd be, picking up trash in the parking lot. We made eye contact and I gave him a thumbs-up, which he returned with a huge smile on his face.

He's not that bad, I thought. *At least he wants to work; he's not lazy.* It reminded me of what my mother had said about him before he became sick—that he'd been a very hard worker. I sat there and chuckled to myself; this was the Jerry everyone had spoken so highly of over the years. He *was* still in there, still holding on.

When it was time for his lunch break, my dad set his tools aside and tore into the aluminum foil covering the food. "Ooh, it smells so good! It's been a long time since I've had home-cooked food."

"I'm glad I was able to make it for you."

"You know, Muffins, a hardworking man should always come home to a good dinner," my dad said, digging into the salad with his fork.

I nodded my head in agreement, watching my dad voraciously devour his lunch.

"So," my dad went on between bites, "you should get home and make sure my son-in-law has dinner."

"Yes, sir."

"Thank you, babygirl."

"You're welcome, Daddy."

I gave him a big hug when he was done eating, gathered the dirty utensils and plates, and drove home while he went back to work.

That night I laid awake thinking about him, and how it'd been our first "normal" day together in such a long time. I decided that if I could be patient, I could still get to know my father—the Jerry everyone talked about. I just had to remain hopeful, waiting for those moments to occur. I pondered on the differences between Jerry and Apple: Apple, the part of my father that possessed no self-control, and often became lost in confusion and paranoia. Then there was Jerry, who was hardworking, proud, and the best thing of all: a fighter. Jerry knew that Apple existed, but he fought against that side of himself—I was witnessing him do so.

As I drifted to sleep, I anticipated how my dad would call me the next day, talking about how he'd scoured that parking lot to ensure every last inch of it was clean.

"You have to spray it with bleach," he'd say, and I'd hum in acknowledgement. "That's how you get rid of all the germs. Because if you clean up without bleach, it's not really clean."

"Of course, Daddy," I'd say, and the admiration in my tone would be honest and true.

• • •

The next morning I woke up to no missed calls from my dad, which worried me a little.

That's weird. Why didn't he call? I wondered as I walked into the kitchen to fry him up some chicken with salad, just the way he liked it. When I drove to Honey Bear's I didn't spot him in the parking lot, so I went inside to order some food.

"Hi, can I take your order?" asked the young cashier from behind the counter.

"Can I have a barbecue chicken with a side of potato salad please?"

"You sure can; anything else?"

"Just a quick question," I said, peering around the busy establishment, "my dad was here cleaning the parking lot yesterday. Is he here today?"

"Let me check for you," the cashier replied, disappearing into the back office for a minute. When she reemerged, her lips were pursed. "I guess he didn't show up today."

"Oh," I said, handing her my credit card to pay for the order. "Thanks for checking for me."

I immediately called George, my dad's Magellan caseworker, and left a voicemail when he didn't answer. I decided to check all of the places where my dad frequented, which were mostly around southern Phoenix where he'd grown up. A lot of people in that area knew our families, and would sometimes give my dad meals and odd jobs to keep him afloat.

I stopped by the Circle K on 16th Street and Southern Avenue first, checking with the homeless people who congregated there about whether they'd seen my dad. They shook their heads, so I went across the street to the smoke shop. I greeted the owner, and he said my dad hadn't been in that morning. Next door was OK Fish & Chips, and beside it the Roots Rasta shop—no one at either location had run into my dad that day. I popped my head inside the barbershop around the corner to no avail, followed by a quick check of the 7-Eleven on 7th Street.

I'd grown increasingly nervous by that time, and marched into the neighborhood on 20th Street and Southern. I stopped by a place nicknamed the "White House," because it was a gigantic white house on the street corner where a lot of locals would hang out. A few people stood outside, tinkering away on an old car.

"Hi, I'm Apple's daughter, Alexis," I said to the nearest man. "I was wondering if you'd seen him this morning?"

"No, not yet! He's usually not around until the evening," the man said.

"Thanks," I said, returning to my car and driving it once more through the neighborhood. I didn't spot my dad anywhere, so I headed to the main road and pulled into a Family Dollar parking lot. *Where could he be?* I thought back to the conversation I'd had with Stephon seven years before, when I'd first went looking for my dad and began learning about the areas homeless people tended to gather in.

With a renewed sense of direction, I exited the car and walked to the back of the Family Dollar building, where I'd seen a homeless camp set up behind some dumpsters a while before.

The camp was still there, but much larger, and it reeked of body odor and trash. The smell was piercing, and stung my nose. As I walked through the camp, I wanted to cover my face to escape the stench, but I didn't so as to avoid offending anyone. Instead, I tried to breathe solely through my mouth, and that helped. I wandered past tents of all colors and sizes, sleeping bags, makeshift stoves, canned goods, and the people who resided there.

The first person to catch my eye was a younger guy, possibly in his mid-twenties like I was. He wasn't as dirty as the others, but his clothing was far too big for his tall, skinny build.

"Hey, do you have a cigarette?" he asked, ambling over on his twig-like legs.

"Yeah," I said, reaching for the newly purchased pack in my purse. Whenever I went to look for my father, I would often buy a pack of Newport's to hand out to those people who gave me clues about his whereabouts.

I handed the guy a cigarette, and he took it with an unsteady hand. I watched him try to light the cigarette with matches, but his hands were too shaky. "Here, take my lighter."

He took it, and I glanced at the black gunk under his short fingernails. Red sores dotted his arms, neck, and a few places on his face. He must've been picking at them recently; several scabs had been torn off, with fresh blood welling up in their wake. I looked into his soft brown eyes, instantly aware of the source of his troubles: meth. *Meth got you, and now you're here.*

"Thank you," he said politely, once he'd successfully lit the cigarette and taken a deep, grateful drag.

"Hey, I'm looking for my dad," I said, giving the young man a brief description of my father's appearance.

He squinted, then frowned. "Haven't seen him."

"Thanks anyway. Here, have another cigarette," I said, which he accepted with a mumbled "thanks." My chest ached for him, but there was nothing more I could do.

Continuing through the camp, I saw an older woman lying on a yoga mat, her dog curled up beside her. There were lots of dogs in the homeless camp, probably for companionship. A couple reclined on a stained mattress reading a book together, and I was calmed by the sight. Even in the midst of all that instability and dysfunction, they'd still found comfort in the written word.

I blocked the sun from my eyes with my hand, scanning the remainder of the camp, when suddenly—*there*. My dad stood in a corner by himself, and was remarkably filthier than he'd been the day before. He was wearing grey sweats, and had a cart piled high with clothes, canned food, and other stuff that he was busily rearranging. He'd go between the cart and a pile of more stuff on the ground, back and forth, back and forth, talking rapidly to himself.

I observed him at first, crossing my arms and leaning against a nearby chain-link fence in silence. When he finally looked my way, his eyes were glassy and unfocused—he was in another world, one in which I didn't exist.

I stood there for fifteen minutes or so, a lump growing in my throat as tears threatened to fall from my eyes. I wanted to go to him, but knew it was best not to interrupt him in such a state. Instead I just whispered a short prayer, asking God to watch over him and keep him safe, and left.

CHAPTER 5

In the following months I toyed with the idea of letting my dad live with me, since it was so hard to watch him on the streets. Honestly, though, I didn't know much about him. He'd never been violent around me or my daughters, but there were still quite a few concerns that needed smoothing out before I'd truly consider it. I knew better than to ask my mom's opinion, as her response would've been a resounding "No!" right away.

One day in the spring of 2012 I asked Stephon if we could go out to dinner at our favorite sushi spot, planning to discuss the possibility of my father moving in then.

Stephon got home from work on time, and we both dressed in nice outfits for a rare night out just the two of us. Once we were sat at our usual table, Stephon reached for the menu.

"So, I've been thinking…" I started, tapping my fingers on the table and sipping from my water glass.

Stephon looked up from the menu and quirked a brow at me. "And?"

"Um…"

"Alexis. *What?*"

"I think maybe we should let my dad stay with us for a bit?" I blurted out.

He dropped the menu on the table, his mouth falling open. "No. Bad idea. *No.*"

"He's homeless though!"

"We can find somewhere else for him to go."

"He needs to be around his family, not with strangers," I said defensively.

"I don't understand why this is even an option. He's schizophrenic, unpredictable, and we have the girls there! It's not going to work."

"I wanna try at least," I implored. "You'll be there, you can step in if anything happens—which I don't think it ever will. *Please.* He's living in a tent, and summer's coming! It'll be too hot for him."

Stephon blinked; Arizona summers could easily reach a fatal 120 degrees, and he knew it. "Fine—a *trial* run."

I clapped my hands together. "Yes! That's a good plan."

I called Vanessa to tell her, and she had no qualms about relaying to me what a horrible idea she thought it all was—but my heart was set on it.

The next morning, Stephon and I set out to find my father. As always, he was hard to locate, but I eventually came across him pushing his cart along Southern Avenue.

"Ugh, he has that damn cart," I muttered, hating how attached he clearly was to it. We pulled up next to him and I rolled down the window and waved. "Daddy!"

His head whipped around until he found us, eyes instantly lighting up with recognition. "Muffins!"

Yes! I cheered inside, *that's the Jerry I know. That's my dad.* I could always tell by the eyes which side of him was present. We parked in a nearby lot and glanced at each other once more.

41

You sure? Stephon's expression asked wordlessly; after more than seven years together parenting our two daughters, we could have whole conversations without uttering a single syllable aloud.

Yeah.

"Hey Muffins," my dad said when he reached us, opening my car door to give me a hug and grinning at Stephon. "Hey son-in-law!"

"Daddy, I have some good news," I said cautiously, as if *I* were the parent preparing to tell my child about an impending move.

"What is it? Are you having another grandbaby?"

"No, that's not it. I want you to come live with us."

"With you?" My father took a step away from the car, seeming almost disappointed.

"Yes. I don't want you living out here on the streets."

"Well…" he wrung his hands, pointing behind him. "What about my cart?"

"What about it?"

"Can I bring my cart to your house?"

"No, you have to leave it here. Don't worry Daddy, I bought you all new stuff," I said, indicating to some Wal-Mart items in the backseat I'd bought earlier.

My father sidled further away. "No, it's okay Muffins."

What? I couldn't believe what he was saying, and it took me a few moments to react when he started on down the street, pushing his cart. I jumped out of the passenger seat and kept pace beside him. "Daddy, please! You can't stay out here, it's getting too hot!"

"Don't you worry Muffins, your dad is a soldier. I've been in this heat my whole life," he replied, wheeling his cart along.

"I know, but it's just not right for you to be living out here." I glanced back at Stephon in desperation, and he shrugged from behind the steering wheel. "Daddy, wait!" I reached in my pocket and grabbed forty dollars. "Here."

My dad stopped and stared at the bills in my palm. "I don't need all that Muffins."

"Please. You should have money to buy something to drink."

He reluctantly took a twenty and shoved it in his pocket.

"Can we give you a ride somewhere?" I asked, still dejected that he'd refused my offer.

"Yeah, to Baseline," my dad said, motioning to a street two lights away. "But what about my cart?"

"We can put it in the trunk."

"All right Muffins, let's do it."

Once the cart was in the trunk—it didn't exactly "fit," but we weren't going far and I could hold onto it from the backseat—I took out my phone and asked my dad for a picture. "Let's take a selfie, Daddy."

He squinted, perplexed. "A what?"

"A selfie! It's just a picture of us; come here."

We took two and they came out perfectly, and then Stephon drove us over to Baseline Road. I wrote my number on an old receipt with some hearts and smiley faces, handing the paper to my dad. "Call me any time."

"Thanks Muffins. You're the only person that loves me," my dad said while Stephon yanked the cart out of the car's trunk, adding the large Wal-Mart bags to the cart's existing items.

"Well, do you love me back?" I teased, clambering out of the car behind my father.

"Muffins, we have the same face," he laughed, leaning in to hug me. "How could I not love you?"

"Be safe and stay hydrated!" I called out a few seconds later, as my dad ambled across the street to a carwash. He wheeled it over to a dumpster and climbed in the cart, bejaginning to rummage through the trash and selecting several things to toss in with his cart's other items. My heart slammed into my stomach when he pulled out some old food and started eating it—I'd just given him twenty bucks!

"Do you want to get him?" Stephon murmured.

"No," I said, exhaling with a resolute shake of my head. "Let's leave him alone."

When I was back in the passenger seat, Stephon grabbed my hand. "You all right?"

"Can we just go?"

"Yep."

I turned to Stephon on our way home, tears distorting my vision into a bleary mix of desert browns and achingly white Arizona sun. "Do you think he could ever be normal, like if he took his medications? That he could just be *Jerry*?"

Stephon cocked his head at me. "Who else would he be?"

"Apple," I said quietly. "The person eating out of the dumpster." I opened the glove compartment, searching for a box of tissues. "Should I keep fighting for Jerry? Or should I just give up? I don't know what to do, and I'm just so tired of this chase."

"It *does* feel like a chase, doesn't it?" Stephon remarked as I buried my face in my hands.

"Yeah," I said between sniffles. "I feel like I'm always chasing Apple to find Jerry."

CHAPTER 6

That night I couldn't sleep, pondering the ways I might find Jerry and keep *him* around. I concluded that if I could provide him with some stability, a home, and medication he'd take regularly, that it might be the key to getting rid of Apple for good.

The next morning I told Stephon about my revised strategy. After he agreed, we dropped our daughters off at my half-sister Shay's house. Shay was younger than me by two years, and we shared a mom. Even though Jerry wasn't her father, she always treated him kindly whenever she saw him, giving him food and water when the opportunity arose. He would never accept her money though; if Shay gave my dad cash, he would hand it right back to her or her son Josiah with a wink. Shay lived ten minutes away from us with her husband and Josiah, and our families were really close.

Once the girls had disappeared inside Shay's house, we were on the hunt for my dad, checking all of his hotspots without success. We'd parked in the 7-Eleven lot to regroup when I suddenly heard someone yelling "Muffins! Muffins!" nearby. I turned in my seat and spotted my dad across the street, waving his arms around.

"What's he doing?" Stephon asked.

"I don't know," I responded as I waved back.

My dad yelled something to me but I couldn't hear him over the traffic, and I shook my head at him. "What, Daddy? I can't hear you!"

He gestured for us to wait, then leapt off the sidewalk in the middle of traffic toward us.

"Dad!" I cried as he dodged honking cars, running through the busy intersection as irate drivers rolled down their windows and cursed at him.

"He's going to get hit!" Stephon said, and I held my breath until my dad had safely crossed and jogged up to our car window. He was shirtless and sopping wet.

"Hey Muffins, hey son-in-law," he wheezed, leaning over to rest his hands on his knees.

"Daddy, why are you wet?"

"Oh, I was just taking a shower behind the Family Dollar." He pointed back the way he'd come.

"How'd you do that?"

"You know—used a bucket, filled it up, and washed myself."

"Hmm. Do you have any clothes to wear?" I asked, crossing my arms.

"Yeah, my shirt's right here," he said, yanking it from his back pocket and wringing it out over the pavement.

"No, Daddy," I said, "like dry, *clean* clothes?"

"Ooh, no Muffins, the sun will dry my clothes."

Stephon and I looked at each other, and I tried not to get upset. *Please agree to stay with me,* I prayed, forcing myself to smile at my father. "Why don't we go to some stores and get you some new clothes, and then we can have dinner at Nessie's house—you can even stay at our place after! What do you think about that?"

"Yeah, that's fine; let me go get my things, all right?"

"Behind the Family Dollar? We'll drive you—"

My dad had already taken off though, straight into oncoming traffic.

"Geez!" I cried as Stephon backed the car up to follow him.

"Are you ready for this Alexis?" he asked, flicking his blinker on to turn into the store's lot. "Your dad is so unpredictable… what about a shelter? Or a mental health facility? You don't think those are better options?"

"No, they're not. He wouldn't stay, for one, and those places aren't well-kept. This is the only way." I unbuckled my seatbelt as Stephon drove over to where my dad stood next to his makeshift camp behind the store, one that was populated by other homeless people who'd set up living arrangements as well. My father had a small tent, two buckets, and his cart, which was draped in more wet clothes.

"Hey Muffins, are you hungry? I have a can of green beans," my dad said when I exited the car to join him.

"I'm not hungry," I said.

"Well, you can give it to my son-in-law," my dad continued, pressing the can into my hands. "And I can't forget my grandbabies." My dad searched through more cans at the bottom of his cart, noisily shoving them around. "They'll like these!" He handed me two cans of fruit cocktail with a satisfied look. "Always give them fruit for something sweet, babygirl. Not that candy, it'll give them cavities."

"Thank you Daddy," I said, taking the canned goods back to the car. *This is a Jerry moment,* I thought, *when he's so sweet and generous.* They were the moments I loved the most, and longed to see more of. Since he was in a relatively lucid state that morning, I felt encouraged about my plan's success. "All right—is there anything you want to take with you?"

"Yeah, Muffins. Everything," my dad stated.

"Everything?"

"Yeah. Hey, son-in-law! Can you help me put the cart in the trunk?"

I grabbed my dad's arm. "No, Daddy, we can't bring the cart."

"I need to keep my stuff somewhere!"

"You'll have a dresser at home," I prodded. "You can put your things in there."

"I don't want to leave my cart," he said sadly.

"How about we get you another cart when we get closer to the apartment?" Stephon said, having joined us beside my father's little camp. "There's a grocery store right around the corner, I can grab you one."

"Really? You'd do that?" my dad asked, instantly cheered.

"Of course. Let's figure it out on the way."

Once we'd put my dad's portable belongings in the car and he was situated in the front seat, we began our errands before heading home. My dad reached for the radio, fiddling with the stations until he found Luniz's "I Got 5 On It." He sang along happily, but his mood soured when we drove through a tunnel and the station turned to static.

"Hey! Hey!" my father yelled, slamming his hands on the dashboard and startling both Stephon and me. "Why isn't this damn thing working?!"

"Hold on Jerry, I got it," Stephon said, weaving between cars in the tunnel until we once again saw the huge blue sky above and the song blared through the speakers.

My dad chuckled and slapped Stephon on the shoulder. "I knew you'd fix it, son-in-law."

I sat in the back, quietly contemplating whether I'd made the right decision.

Our first stop was a department store to get my dad some tasteful new outfits. People there gave us disgusted looks and my dad talked so loudly he was practically yelling, but I didn't care—I was just thankful he'd allowed us to take him there.

As we waited in the checkout line, my dad began to cry. "Thank you so much son-in-law," he said in between sobs, leaning on Stephon's shoulder.

"No problem Jerry, happy to help," Stephon said with a gentle pat.

My dad lifted his head and wiped his eyes. "You know, when I get a job, I'm going to pay you back, I'm going to do a whole one-eighty, and then I'll take *you* shopping."

On the way to our apartment, I called Vanessa to confirm we could all come over for dinner at six. My dad was excited for her planned meal of enchiladas with rice and beans, and he chattered away as we pulled into the complex's lot.

"So you can shower while we get you settled in," I said, leading my dad inside our place. "We'll pick up the girls on the way to Nessie's."

My dad whistled, circling around with admiration. "You're living the life, Muffins!"

"Here, let me show you your room." He followed me into the girls' bedroom, which we'd decided to give him for his stay; Alexandra and Aubrey would sleep on an air mattress in the living room. "And here's the bathroom, where you can get cleaned up," I explained as he followed me into the hallway.

"Ay ay captain!" my dad said with a comical salute. "I'll be in there for a while—I want to look my best for my grandkids and Vanessa."

After I'd turned the shower on and placed a new outfit on the sink for him, I shut the bathroom door and rejoined

Stephon in the living room. He was seated on the couch rubbing his temples.

"Headache?" I asked, sitting beside him.

"No." Stephon removed his hands, and his eyes were downcast. "He can't stay here."

I bristled, immediately defensive. "Why?"

"It's not going to work," he whispered forcibly. "I don't have a good feeling about this."

"He's homeless!" I pleaded as Stephon pushed up from the couch to stand over me.

"I get that, but I'm worried about leaving you and the girls alone with him when I'm at work. He needs to go after dinner *tonight*."

My anger flared at Stephon's sudden change of heart, and I rose to dig my phone out of my purse. "Stephon, it's gonna be fine! I'll call Shay and see if the girls can stay the night with her, okay?"

When I ended the call with Shay, I found Stephon in the hallway with his ear against the bathroom door. He signaled for me to be join him, and I tiptoed over.

"What?" I hissed.

"Just listen!"

"Okay Lorayne, I'm going to work now. I'll come for you and Tyrue after I get off," my dad said from inside the bathroom.

I swallowed down the concern gathering at the base of my throat; he was talking to himself again, and it was admittedly unnerving. "Come on, we shouldn't be spying on him—"

The door swung open and my dad locked eyes with us, dressed in his new clothes. "Son-in-law! I look just as good as you!" He stepped out to join us in the hall, extending his arms and swinging from side to side.

Stephon laughed a bit nervously since we'd been caught snooping, but either my dad didn't realize it or he didn't care. "Yes you do, Jerry. Very nice. Ready to go?"

"Yes, I want to see my grandbabies."

"Let me lock up and we can head out," I said, avoiding Stephon's *this isn't over* stare. *He just doesn't understand.*

Once we'd all climbed into the car, my dad asked Stephon about getting another cart, which annoyed me. He had a clean place to stay, nice clothes, a shower…who gave a crap about a stupid cart?

We stopped to get our daughters from Shay's, who'd agreed when we spoke to take them back after dinner for the night. She was waiting outside with Alexandra, Aubrey, and Josaiah as we pulled up.

"Grandbabies!" my dad yelled as we parked the car and got out. He reached down into his pockets, pulling out two one-dollar bills and some change. He handed Alexandra and Josaiah one dollar each, and Aubrey the change.

"Jerry, thank you, but I just gave Josaiah his allowance for doing chores," Shay said kindly, trying to return the money to him.

"No, no," he said, wrapping an arm around Josaiah's slim shoulders. "I don't take money from my grandchildren. I'm happy to give him something."

"We'll be back after dinner," I whispered to Shay while my dad played with the kids.

She nodded, her thin eyebrows scrunching into a frown. "You *sure* you wanna do this? What if things go bad?"

I shrugged. "Then they go bad. But I can't just stand by and do nothing anymore."

We said our goodbyes, and headed off to Vanessa's house. On the ride there, my dad asked Stephon if he could drive.

"Do you have a license?" I asked.

"No," my dad answered, clearly unsure of why that mattered.

"Well it's a no from me then!" Stephon laughed.

"Oh come on, son-in-law!" my dad needled. "Let me drive!"

"Daddy, we're already here," I said, pointing to Vanessa's house on the corner. Her kids were outside playing, and Alexandra and Aubrey leapt out of the car to go greet their cousins.

"I'm gonna pick up some drinks at the store—you want anything?" Stephon asked.

I declined and exited the car with my dad, following the girls up the walkway.

"Thanks for having us," I said to Vanessa on her front porch, punctuating the statement with an enthusiastic embrace.

"Of course. It's good to see you. Hi Dad," Vanessa said, also hugging our father. They'd smoothed things over since that day many years before when he'd cursed in her face, but a nest of anxiety always slithered in my gut when they were together.

I helped Vanessa set the table while keeping a close eye on our dad, who was in the front yard pretending to be a monster and chasing the kids across the lawn.

"Do you honestly think he's going to be fine staying at your place?" Vanessa asked as she spooned rice into a bowl. "I don't have a good feeling about this. I think you should take him back."

I snorted. "It's too late, Nessie! He's already agreed. I'll call them in for dinner."

After everyone had come inside, washed their hands, and were seated to eat, my dad leaned over and spoke in my ear. "Muffins?"

"Yeah?"

"I really need my cart."

"Okay. After we eat, we'll get you a cart."

Vanessa passed me my plate and mouthed "Take him back," but I ignored it.

"Can I have one now?" my dad implored, his knee jiggling rapidly under the table.

"Don't you want to eat?" I said, trying to keep my voice level.

"No I don't."

"Nessie made this dinner for you, we all wanted to have a nice meal—"

"Well I don't want to eat!" he yelled suddenly, "I want my fucking cart!"

"All right," I said, raising my hands to try and calm him. "When the kids are done eating and Stephon gets back from the store, we'll go."

My dad shot up from his chair and stormed out the back door, and I looked at the kids around the table. "Grandpa's not in a good mood tonight, but it's gonna be okay. Eat your dinner, everything's fine."

I followed after my dad and stood in the doorway with Vanessa, both of us watching him pace and throw punches in the air, fighting some invisible foe.

My half-sister retreated, pulling me with her. "Alexis, I'm scared. I want him gone—now."

I called Stephon and explained what was happening.

"I'm on my way," he said into the receiver, his breath audibly hitched as he finished his purchase and jogged back to the car.

"Hurry," I said, hanging up and going out to the backyard to stand beside my dad. "Hey Daddy," I said in the most cheerful tone I could muster, "We're gonna leave in about five minutes."

"Are you gonna take me to my cart?" my dad asked, wild-eyed.

"*Yes,*" I ground out, almost failing to keep my composure.

"Okay Muffins, it's just really important that I get back to my cart."

"Yeah, I get it, you need your cart. Do you wanna say goodbye to Nessie's kids?"

My father went back inside and hugged each kid, repeating "It's not goodbye, it's see you later" several times.

"Grandpa loves you," he said when Stephon had returned and we were ready to go. "I'll come back soon—remember, it's always see you later, never goodbye. I'll see you later Vanessa."

"Yeah, see you," she said, giving him a one-armed hug.

I hustled Alexandra and Aubrey into the car and we brought them to Shay's for the night. My father was mercifully silent about his cart until it was just him, me, and Stephon inside.

"We're going to my cart right?" my dad asked immediately after the girls had disembarked.

"Yes!" I barked, staring out the backseat window. My patience had frayed to a thread—there I was, offering my dad *everything* he needed to get better, and he couldn't think of anything but a damn shopping cart!

We stopped at the apartment to pick up the toiletries and clothing we'd purchased for my dad, then returned to the Family Dollar where we'd gotten him earlier that day. It began to rain on the way, and I leaned against the headrest. *Great—as if I didn't already feel bad about dropping him off.*

When we arrived at the Family Dollar, my dad started bouncing excitedly in his seat. "My cart, my cart, there it is!" he squealed, tapping his hands on the dashboard.

"We all see the fucking cart!" I bellowed. Seeing him rejoice over that ridiculous shopping cart angered my soul, and I was *done* holding my emotions in.

When Stephon eased the car to a stop my dad scrambled out, running over to where his cart and tent were still sitting.

I went after him, squinting into the pouring rain. "Do you have an umbrella?!"

"No," he said, maneuvering his cart closer to his tent and moving his buckets around. "I don't need one."

"Let's go buy you one so you don't get all wet."

"No, it's okay Muffins."

At that moment, there under the warm downpour of a Phoenix monsoon, I lost it. "Why? *Why* is it okay for you to get all wet in the fucking rain?! WHY?!"

"Muffins, it doesn't bother me."

"Are you kidding me right now? How can it not bother you?!" I exploded, flapping my arms around in rage. "How can it not bother you that you're sleeping in a fucking tent behind a fucking dollar store?! You're sleeping behind a Family Dollar, don't you *see* the Family Dollar sign right there? This is a *store*, not a place of residence! People buy their clothes and food here, they don't *live behind it*!"

By that point other homeless people in the camp had begun to emerge from their tents and makeshift shelters, watching me make a fool of myself. "Do you know where people *really* live, Daddy?! They live in houses, apartments, and condos; not behind stores, because it's not okay." I spun around, pining every homeless person with my stare. "It's not okay for any of you to be out here! You shouldn't be living in tents—" I reached for my dad's small tent and tore at it so hard that it collapsed "—and it's not acceptable to be eating from the trash!" I took one of my dad's cans out of his cart and threw it to the ground, stepping on it aggressively so that it dented under my shoe.

"Alexis! Alexis, what are you doing?!" Stephon said, emerging from the car and rushing over.

"And you know what's *really* not okay?!" I continued, undeterred. "Huh?! Do you?! It's not okay to push around these stupid carts!"

I kicked at my dad's cart and it tipped dangerously to the side, then fell so that his cans and belongings tumbled onto the wet pavement.

"Alexis!" Stephon repeated, picking me up from behind and dragging me back to the car. My dad stared after me in shock, and I was positively vibrating with fury.

"None of this is okay!" I said as Stephon held me against the passenger door.

"What are you doing?!" he said, gripping my cheeks between his palms. I'd begun to cry, and I blinked against the rain as I finally returned to my senses.

Other homeless people had started to help my dad gather his things and place them back in the cart, and a few others were putting his tent back together. I was inundated by embarrassment and regret; I'd never lost control of myself like that.

I stepped around Stephon and picked up a can that had rolled far away, then held it out to my dad. "I'm sorry," I murmured, "I'm sorry Daddy."

My father wouldn't return my gaze as he accepted the can and placed it among the others. "I'm sorry," I said again, all three of us standing there in the drizzle. My dad didn't reply, instead walking over to Stephon and extending a hand to shake it. "Thank you, son-in-law."

"No problem man," Stephon answered gently.

"See you later." My dad walked past me without saying a word, and I trailed after him.

"Daddy, I'm really sorry, I just lost my temper—I want you to be okay! I don't want you living out here, that's it." I reached out and grabbed his arm, but he flinched away.

"Okay Alexis."

Alexis? He never called me that.

My dad went to his cart and started to push it through the camp, and I called after him. "I understand you're mad right now, so I'll just see you later!"

"Bye Alexis," he said over his shoulder.

"I thought it wasn't goodbye—it's see you later!"

My dad didn't respond, and I stood there in the rain, defeated.

I give up, I thought, glancing over at Stephon, who'd opened the car door for me. His expression was as somber as mine must've been, and we drove home in silence.

CHAPTER 7

T he next morning I called Vanessa to tell her about what had happened.

"Hello?" she said groggily; I was an early riser, but my half-sister certainly wasn't.

"You up?" I asked.

"I am *now*. What's going on?"

"So…I had a little meltdown last night at dad's homeless camp." Vanessa started to laugh as I explained everything, and by the end of it, we were both in hysterics.

"You lost it, huh?! You really lost it!" she said between giggles. "Wow. It was only a matter of time."

We chatted about our dad some more, and concluded that there was no forcing him to do something he didn't want to do. "The best thing is to just leave him alone, Alexis," Vanessa said, and I reluctantly agreed.

After we hung up, I stared at the ceiling, contemplating my situation. I had to accept it; realistically speaking, it wasn't going to change. It was how my dad had been living for years, and no matter how much I loved him, that alone wouldn't alter his mindset. The best way I could show my care would be through providing him with the necessities, and checking on him regularly. *I've done the best I could,* I mused as I crawled out of bed. *My dad has to know that I love him.*

When I'd first found out about my dad's schizophrenia diagnosis, I'd wondered what it was like for him to live in such a strange reality. What did he see? What did he hear? Were his voices nice to him? One of the YouTube videos I'd watched back then had always stayed with me, of the journalist Anderson Cooper trying out a schizophrenia simulator. After putting on a set of headphones, he'd tried to complete several small tasks while various voices spoke to him, some yelling and aggressive, others low and repetitive. Within seconds of the video, Cooper had become discouraged and said he couldn't complete the origami he'd been trying to make. He said that he wanted to talk back to the voices and tell them to be quiet, so he could have some peace.

Two weeks after my outburst, I went looking for my dad to apologize. After an hour of checking all of his regular hangouts with no results, I stopped at a convenience store and purchased four bottles of water and Top, the tobacco my dad liked to use in his rolled cigarettes.

I sat in my car and dialed my dad's caseworker at Magellan to see if he'd heard anything.

"Alexis? Yeah, your dad was admitted to the hospital for chest pains. He's been in there for about four days now," George said.

In that moment it felt like my heart shuddered to a full stop. "What?! Which hospital?"

After George gave me the name, I ran out of the apartment and sped over there. I sprinted to the front desk and gave my dad's name, and once they'd looked up his room number I found the closest elevator and dove inside. Once it'd reached the third floor and the elevator doors glided open, I immediately heard yelling.

"Get the fuck out!" someone hollered as I exited the elevator and spun to see a stainless steel bedpan go flying through the doorway of one of the hospital rooms.

I didn't need to read the placard on the wall beside the door to know my dad was in there. I went inside and saw him sitting on the bed with a sheet over his head, while a nurse stood beside him with a bag of clear IV fluids in hand.

"I'm so sorry, hi, I'm Alexis," I said to her, hoping to defuse the situation. "Daddy, hey, it's Muffins, I'm here—"

"Get out of here Muffins!" he cried, still not removing the sheet from his face.

"Daddy, I just wanted to check on you—"

"*Get out!*"

I did as he requested, speaking with several members of the nursing staff about his current condition. He was being treated for the dehydration that had caused his chest pains, and was also receiving four milligrams of Risperdal, an antipsychotic, for his schizophrenia.

The nurse informed me that the next day my father would be transferred to a locked behavioral unit for an extended stay "until his medication was at a therapeutic level." I cringed at the thought of my father being locked up, since he was so used to roaming the streets and doing his own thing. I left the hospital without saying goodbye to avoid upsetting him, instead planning to call him later and explain what was to come.

I knew it was going to be a hard few days for my dad, so I stopped at the store on the way home and bought some groceries to make his favorite meal. I got everything to make fried pork chops and an onion and tomato salad, as well as a few of his other beloved goodies: Coca-Cola, pork rinds, and Nescafé's Taster's Choice instant coffee.

I tried to call my dad that night but he didn't answer, so I got up really early the next morning to prepare my dad's food. I packed it all up and headed to the behavioral health unit, and when I entered the facility, their security immediately stopped me to rummage through the bags.

"We need to make sure there's nothing in here he can harm himself with," the security guard explained to me, and I nodded as he removed a can of Vienna sausages and told me the lid was a safety hazard and it couldn't go in. Once the rest of the food had been transferred from plastic bags to paper ones, the guard handed them back to me and told me to put my phone and purse in one of their lockers.

The all-male staff was tall, muscular, and wore solid black uniforms as if they were bouncers at a club and not techs at a behavioral health hospital. The lobby was empty except for me, and I had to go through a metal detector and past two more security guards to reach the elevators. Once I'd stepped inside and pressed the button for the fifth floor, I began to feel nervous about seeing my dad. It was the first time I'd be with him in a controlled setting, and I imagined my dad wearing a straitjacket in a room with padded walls, like on TV.

Ding! It was my stop. *Here we go.* The doors opened and I hesitated for a moment, then slowly walked through the hallway and turned to my left like the front desk attendant had told me to do. I strode up to two double doors and read the sign beside them: "See the nurse before entering." I glanced toward the nurses' station, where four of them sat behind a wall of protective glass.

"Hello, I'm here to see my father," I said to the nearest nurse.

"What's your father's name?"

"Jerry James."

"Is that bag for him?"

I held up the paper bags. "Yes, this is just food."

"Okay, we have to keep it back here. He'll be allowed to eat those items at snack time and meal time." She slid open a little side door and I handed her the bags.

She checked inside a few of them and gasped. "This is a lot of food! You know, we do have meals available here."

"I know," I said, "I just wanted him to have his favorite things."

"That's very sweet." She studied me with a smile, and I noted how white and straight her teeth were. "You must be his daughter; I can see the resemblance."

"Yep, I'm his daughter Alexis. How's he been doing so far?" I asked, peering beyond the station to the other side, where patients were sitting at tables playing cards or watching TV.

"Well…I think he's doing about as good as to be expected. He hasn't left his room," the nurse said.

"Hmm. Is it okay for me to bring his lunch to him? It's some salad and a pork chop," I asked, hoping they might lift my dad's spirits.

The nurse pursed her lips, thinking, but finally agreed. "Sure."

"Did he at least go out for a smoke break?"

The nurse shook her head. "Oh, no—this is a non-smoking facility."

"Seriously?" I said with a frown. "Is there a sitting area outside?"

"No ma'am. They can't go outside."

Now I was *really* close to losing it, but I managed to keep a straight face. *He can't smoke and he can't go outside…those things alone will drive him crazy.*

"Come on in and I'll get your dad," the nurse said, pressing a button so that the double doors buzzed and I could enter. I went inside and she handed me the bag with his lunch, showing me to an open table. "Your father's going to do great here," she said, squeezing my shoulder.

We'll see about that, I thought, beginning to unwrap his meal and dress his salad.

"Muffins!" I heard my father exclaim a minute later.

I stood and prepared to greet him, but he'd already barreled into me so hard with a hug that I fell against the table. "Hey Daddy—whoa!"

"Oh Muffins, I'm so glad to see you, you've gotta get me out of here," he said, gripping my arms and staring into my eyes. "I need to get back to my cart."

"Daddy, look! I made you some pork chops."

"Muffins, you didn't have to. How's your mom? Man, I sure do miss Lorayne—do you think she'll take me back?"

"Probably not, Daddy. Here, eat your salad."

"Aw, Muffins. I want my family back," my dad said, grabbing his fork and beginning to eat. "How're Vanessa and Tyrue?"

"They're fine," I said, sprinkling some of his favorite hot sauce over the pork chop. "Go ahead Daddy, you need to eat something—"

Another patient walked by our table and my dad suddenly shot up. "Don't look at my daughter!" he shouted, startling the other patient, who'd not been paying any attention to us.

A behavioral tech came over and stood between the two men, taller and much larger than either of them. "Mr. James, that's enough. Enjoy the lunch your daughter brought you, okay? I bet it's delicious."

My dad conceded to sit. "Yeah, my Muffins can cook, just like Mrs. Juanita," he said, mentioning my maternal grandmother's culinary prowess as usual. "Thank you Muffins."

"You're welcome Daddy," I said, watching him eat and noting how frail he looked under the fluorescent lights.

My dad's eyes shifted around, and he lowered his voice to a whisper. "We have to think of a plan to get me out. Through the window, maybe?"

"There aren't any windows Daddy."

"Hmm. I could dress up like one of those techs and sneak out. Come on Muffins, you need to help me! Do something useful for once."

I bristled at the harshness in his tone, and crossed my arms. That was Apple talking, and I didn't have the patience for it. "Daddy, I've gotta go. I've got work," I lied; it was a weekday, and I still only worked doubles on the weekends. "I brought some other food for you, and they said you can get it during mealtimes."

We hugged, and my dad didn't release me at first. "Muffins, don't leave me here," he begged in my ear. "They're going to kill me."

"Daddy," I said firmly, disentangling myself, "you are safe here. I'll see you again soon, okay?"

"Muffins please don't go, don't leave me with these people," he continued, clasping my hand so tightly it was uncomfortable.

"I wouldn't leave you here if you weren't safe," I assured him, trying to pull my hand away.

"Muffins," my dad said, louder, "If you leave me here they'll kill me. They'll kill me!" I hurried away from the table and he pursued, repeating the statement until it was a scream. He leapt at me, snatching my wrist until I yelped in pain.

At least five staff members descended on my dad, forcing him to release me and shouting "Formation code red!" as a nurse approached with restraints.

"I'll be back Daddy, I promise," I said, my voice cracking as I backed away. My wrist was throbbing, and red welts were already rising in the shape of his fingers along my skin.

"MUFFINS, PLEASE!" he shrieked, and I saw the real fear in his face—he truly believed he was going to be killed.

"I'll call and check on you," I whimpered, "you're going to be okay. I'm sorry Daddy." My heart raced and I swallowed down my tears as I left, my dad's desperate pleas echoing through the double doors and down the hallway as I hurried toward the elevator.

Once back inside my car, I grasped the steering wheel with trembling hands and rested my head against it as the sobs took over. I couldn't stop recalling the betrayal in my father's expression as I'd left him there in the hospital, and it made me sick to my stomach. My wrist was really starting to hurt, but I knew he hadn't meant to injure me during his episode.

On the drive home I received a call from one of the nurses with an update that he'd been given medication to help him relax, and was now in bed. I thanked her for the update, and said I probably wouldn't be back until the following week.

"That's fine honey," she said. "He'll be okay here, you just take some 'me' time."

The following day I stopped at a thrift store and purchased some clothes for him, and left them at the front desk of the hospital with a note.

Hey Daddy,

*Couldn't stay today, but I'll see you next Wednesday.
Call if you need anything.*

*See you later,
Muffins*

Later that evening, I received a call from an unknown number.

"Hello?" I said, stirring the pasta on the stove while my daughters got situated at the dinner table.

"Muffins!"

"Hi Daddy."

"I need you to get me out of here."

I immediately hung up the phone. *I'm not doing this with him right now.*

My phone vibrated again, and I ignored it. Throughout the night my dad called me twenty-two more times and left fourteen voicemails, all of which I deleted without listening to them. I was mentally exhausted, and didn't have the energy to keep reliving the same conversation when there was nothing I could do to help.

A week passed and I didn't go see my father, nor did I answer his phones calls. By the third week my father had stopped calling me, so I finally reached out to the facility. The nurse on staff told me my father had had a few outbursts where he'd flipped tables over and thrown things at the staff, but informed me that he was doing better.

"I'm sure he'd love to see you," she said. "He talks about you all the time."

I'd had enough time to decompress after our last interaction, so I told her I'd be in shortly. On the way, I stopped at

Church's Chicken to bring something for my dad, and went through the entire process of security, lockers, and elevators.

As I stepped out of the elevator and approached the double doors, I stopped and leaned against the wall, overcome with dread and pure exhaustion over chasing him for all these years. "I can't deal with this anymore," I breathed, clutching the food in one hand and wiping my tears with the other. In that moment, I felt like nothing in his world would ever be okay, no matter what I did.

Someone touched my shoulder and I looked up to see the nurse from my first visit handing me a box of tissues. "Here you go honey," she said, helping me to stand and flashing her beautiful white teeth at me. "I know it's a lot right now."

I nodded in agreement as I dried my face. "Is he okay?"

"Yes he is. We're taking good care of him. He's such a sweet man, and he adores you. It's only when he turns into that ugly person that we don't know—"

"Apple."

"What honey?"

"That person is Apple."

"Ahh," she said, "that's what you call him."

"Yeah," I said, dissolving into tears once more. "I have to deal with Apple to know Jerry. I hate Apple, I just *hate* him."

"I'll give you a moment," the nurse said, leaving me to gather myself. Once I was calmer I went to the window, showed the nurses the Church's Chicken container, and waited to be buzzed in. "He's watching TV in the main room," the friendly nurse said, and I wiped my cheeks once more to make sure they were tear-free.

I scanned the room looking for my father, and heard his soft mumble from the corner.

"Muffins?"

He was seated alone in a chair, and I immediately noticed that something was off about him.

"Hey Daddy. I brought you some chicken." I showed him the Styrofoam container and he tried to smile, but his mouth seemed...*lopsided.*

"You didn't forget about your ol' dad." My father's words were jumbled and irregular, like it was too difficult for him to fully enunciate each one. He was slouched in his chair, and only had one sock on. "You didn't have to bring me food, but it sure does smell good."

I was troubled by his disheveled appearance and drugged state, and tried to help him sit up higher so he could eat. He couldn't seem to keep his balance, so I asked a behavioral tech for a pillow. When he was further upright with a pillow propping him up, I set the food in front of him.

"Thank you Muffins. You're so sweet...that's why you're my Muffins," he slurred, chewing so slowly that the chicken fell out of his mouth. I reached for a napkin and cleaned him up, shocked at the amount of medication they'd put my father on. *He's basically a zombie.*

"How's Lorayne?" my dad said, a trail of drool dribbling from his lips onto his shirt.

I was horrified by this new version of him—sure, Apple was gone, but in his place was a lifeless shell. "Daddy, why don't we pack up your food for later? You look tired; how about I help you to bed?"

My dad blinked his glassy eyes at me and agreed, so I called for another tech and we helped him to his room. I gave my dad a hug, and felt a little better when he managed to say, "It's not goodbye, Muffins. It's see you later."

"See you later Daddy," I said, kissing his cheek once he'd laid down. On my way to the exit, I stopped at the nurses' station. "Who's in charge of Jerry James?"

"I have him for this shift," said one of the nurses I'd never seen before, a thin woman with blonde hair so stiff and immovable it looked like it could withstand hurricane-level winds.

"I think you have him on too many meds," I said. "He can barely function."

"No, no, he's doing so well. The side effects are noticeable, but his behavior has been great," she said, retrieving my dad's chart from a stack and reading over it.

"He doesn't *have* any behaviors!" I snapped. "All he can do is sit there and drool!"

The nurse blinked slowly at me, her smile never wavering. "Well, he'll be out in a week."

I rolled my eyes, irritated by her nonchalance. "*Thanks.*"

It'd been such a difficult few months with my father—all the versions of him—that I wasn't sure either of us would be ready when it came time for his release.

CHAPTER 8

Three weeks passed before I saw my dad again after that last day in the hospital. I'd been so traumatized by witnessing him in such a drugged state that I couldn't bring myself to go looking for him, and a part of me wanted to wait until he was back to his regular self—even if that meant interacting with Apple most of the time.

When another search commenced on an evening in early August, I stopped at Ms. White's Café first and spotted my dad across the street, pushing his cart. His clothes were clean and he seemed healthy, and I rolled my car window down to greet him.

"Daddy!"

He spun until he located me, and waved. "Muffins! Muffins!"

"Meet me in the café parking lot!"

My dad nodded and walked across the street with the cart, stopping in front of my window. We both smiled, and I was relieved to see his faculties had returned; he was no longer a drooling vegetable.

"Hey Daddy, you hungry?" I asked him.

"Hell yeah Muffins. I haven't eaten yet today."

"Okay Daddy, get in."

"Just a sec, let me put my cart away."

My dad hastened behind the café, left the cart near the dumpster, and came back to stand by my door.

"Let me drive, Muffins."

I shook my head at him. "Do you have a license?"

"I don't need one, I'm a grown man!"

"To drive this car you do!" I said, pointing to the empty passenger seat.

"*Fine.*" My dad walked around the car with a huff and got in.

"I'm glad you're free, Daddy," I said, patting his hand.

"Me too Muffins. Me too."

We sat there quietly for a few minutes, just enjoying each other's company. "Where should we go?" I eventually asked.

"You pick."

"Do you want chicken?"

"I can always eat chicken."

"Church's?"

"Okay Muffins."

We headed to the restaurant, and my dad washed up in the bathroom while I ordered. I chose our table and sat down with our drinks, waiting for my dad to join me. When he did, he gathered me close for a long hug.

"Thanks for always coming back for me Muffins," he said into my hair.

"I'll always come back for you Daddy."

"Order number thirty-seven!" screeched someone over the intercom.

"That's us," I said, pulling away to see huge tears glistening on his round cheeks.

"I love you Muffins," he said between sniffles.

"I do too," I replied, meaning it.

While we ate, my dad talked about my mom and I listened, resting my chin in my palm. *I enjoy these times the most,* I thought. When he talked about my mom, he always had the biggest smile, and when he spoke of me, his beloved Muffins,

I could see straight to his loving heart through his eyes. He was thankful for me, and I was thankful for him—this was our fight, and one we weren't going to give up on.

We finished our dinner and began the drive back to Ms. White's Café, with my dad rolling one of his cigarettes on the way.

"Well Muffins, you showed your ol' dad a good time tonight," he said, lighting the cigarette's end and taking a deep drag.

"That was the plan, Daddy."

"I'm getting old," he said, blowing smoke out the window into the balmy night air.

"I know."

"I just have to make sure Lorayne is okay, and you kids too."

"We're fine Daddy."

"Hey," he said, and I met his gaze. "I've got some accounts overseas for you guys. Your ol' dad has it under control."

I nodded and turned into the café's parking lot. "Thanks Daddy."

"Just let me know when you want me to get that money for you, and I will."

I eased the car to a stop beside my dad's cart beside the dumpster and turned to him. "I will. Thanks Daddy."

You know what, Muffins? I'm gonna get a job and make a one-eighty. You just watch."

"That's great Daddy," I said, reaching out for another embrace. "See you later."

"See you later Muffins," he said, climbing out and going straight for his cart. I watched him push it to the street corner, wait for the light to change, and then cross, and I kept staring until I could only make out his silhouette getting smaller and smaller, until it completely disappeared.

I never discouraged my dad from his dreams, and I never told him they wouldn't come true. If he was able to cling to some semblance of hope through all of the difficulty and struggle he'd endured, I certainly wasn't going to take that away from him. Because if he could do it, then so could I.

I would like to express a special thank you to my friend George for guiding me through the guardianship process with my father. And to the owners and employees of Mrs. White's Golden Rule Cafe for their generosity, compassion, and humility showed towards my father

Thank you.

Alexis Reed, author of "Chasing Apple to Find Jerry" is a dedicated nurse in Phoenix, AZ. She is the founder of "Apple Seeds" which provides meals to the unsheltered population throughout the Valley.

Made in the USA
Las Vegas, NV
27 April 2022

48082860R00052